100

THINGS TO DO IN
ORLANDO
BEFORE YOU
DIE

2nd Edition

100

THINGS TO DO IN
ORLANDO
BEFORE YOU
DIE

• •

JOHN BROWN & JON BUSDEKER

REEDY PRESS

Library of Congress Control Number: 2018945629

ISBN: 9781681061610

Design by Jill Halpin

Cover photo by Jim Hobart of Macbeth Studio

Printed in the United States of America
18 19 20 21 22 5 4 3 2 1

Please note that websites, phone numbers, addresses, and company names are subject to change or cancellation. We did our best to relay the most accurate information available, but due to circumstances beyond our control, please do not hold us liable for misinformation. When exploring new destinations, please do your homework before you go.

DEDICATION

To Teresa, Lauren and Sophie, my partners for
adventure all over Central Florida.
—John Brown

To my wife LeAnn and my Mom and Dad,
thank you for always believing in me.
—Jon Busdeker

• •

CONTENTS

● ●

• •

Culture and History

• •

• •

PREFACE

When the first edition of this book was published in 2014, the Orlando metro area touted some amazing tourism numbers. That year, more than fifty-four million visitors came to Central Florida to take part in all the amazing adventures this area has to offer. That was the first year Orlando passed New York City as the number one tourist destination in the United States. Three years later, we welcomed a record seventy-two million visitors. That averages out to about 1.4 million guests every single week, which is about half the resident population of Central Florida! That means a whole new group of people needs a manual to find the "must see" destinations, which is exactly what this book is about.

100 Things to Do in Orlando started out as a compilation of all the fun things I showcased during my time as a TV show host with WOFL-Fox 35 and on *The Daily Buzz*, a nationally syndicated show based in Orlando. When we decided to do a second edition, it was only logical to have a coauthor who also spends his time exploring Central Florida attractions. Jon Busdeker has profiled many of these destinations as a writer for the *Orlando Sentinel*; a TV reporter at WESH-2, Central Florida's NBC affiliate; the founder of *Orlando 60*; and the cohost of *Bungalower and The Bus* on Real Radio 104.1-FM. This book is a great blend of all the things we think you need to do in Central Florida during your lifetime, and, trust us, it could take a lifetime to do everything there is to do across this metro area.

● ●

Think of this book as your "bucket list." We of course profile the world-class theme parks in Orlando and tell you how to experience them like a "rock star," but there is more to Orlando than the parks. We take you to hidden destinations, indoor activities, underwater attractions, and things you can only experience in a place this special. You may have done some of these, but we guarantee there will be some new ideas for you to explore in Central Florida.

One of the most rewarding comments I received after the first edition of this book was published went something like this: "I've lived here my entire life and never knew that existed." So, whether you are new to the area or a Florida native, we hope you find something new and wonderful to experience in this book. This is the greatest state, with some of the best people you will find anywhere. We hope you are able to experience the Sunshine State in new ways and see the many reasons we call Orlando "The City Beautiful."

—John Brown
September 2018

· ·

FOOD AND DRINK

GO TO WINE COUNTRY,
FLORIDA STYLE

Florida has always been known for fresh fruits, but grapes don't normally come to mind. But Lake County is home to Lakeridge Winery, one of the few working wineries in the state of Florida. The tour of the winery is cool enough, but you can add another notch to the fun factor during one of the festivals. You and the children can even take part in a grape stomp right there on the rolling hills of Lake County. You will see how the wines are made, get a sample (or two), and—during the Summer Concert Series—hear a local band playing outside in the shade.

19239 US 27
Clermont, FL 34715
(352) 394-8627
lakeridgewinery.com

TIP
If you like wine and chocolate, the Wine and Chocolate Festival is held in mid-December.

OTHER WINERIES AND DISTILLERIES IN THE ORLANDO AREA

Keel and Curley Winery, Plant City
keelandcurleywinery.com

Palm Ridge Reserve Distillery, Umatilla
palmridgereserve.com

Winter Park Distilling, Winter Park
wpdistilling.com

Quantum Leap Winery, Orlando
quantumleapwinery.com

Hutchinson Farm Winery, Apopka
hutchinsonfarmwinery.com

GET A TASTE OF THE OLD FLORIDA
AT DAVIDSON OF DUNDEE

Going to Davidson of Dundee is sort of like taking a trip back in time. Dating to the 1960s, this roadside attraction in Polk County is what tourists encountered before the days of Walt Disney World and Universal Orlando. Jams, jellies, marmalades, chocolates, and old-fashioned citrus-flavored candies are the main attraction at Davidson of Dundee. The family-run business, which doubles as a gift shop, makes all its products one batch at a time, and you can watch the process. Here's the best part: All visitors get a free sample!

28421 Hwy. 27
Dundee, FL 33838
(863) 439-1698
davidsonofdundee.com

TIP
If you visit Davidson of Dundee and forget to buy a jar of jelly or a box of candies, you can still purchase the items online and have them shipped right to your house.

GET YOUR SUGAR ON
AT NORA'S SUGAR SHACK

You know how everyone on the TV show *Cheers* knows your name? Nora's Sugar Shack in the Ivanhoe Village district of Orlando is sort of like that . . . only a lot funkier. This wine shop/beer store/ cigar shop/drinking establishment is an Orlando institution and a great spot for a drink. Owner Nora Brooker is a unique character, and that's what makes her shop so special. She may give you a hug when you walk in, and you may get to meet her dogs, which roam around the shop on most nights. Nora's Sugar Shack is inside an old bungalow, so when you're sipping an IPA or a glass of pinor noir, it really does feel like you're in her living room.

636 Virginia Dr.
Orlando, FL 32803
(407) 447-5885
noraswinecigars.com

DRINK BEER
LIKE A LOCAL

In the past several years, the Orlando area has become a beer lover's destination. More than seventeen breweries and even more specialty beer bars can be found in Central Florida. Some of the highlights include Orlando Brewing, Ten10 Brewing, Crooked Can Brewing Company, Red Cypress Brewing Company, Persimmon Hollow Brewing Company, and Broken Cauldron Taproom. And don't miss Redlight, Redlight. Not only does the watering hole in the Audubon Park Garden District in Orlando have one of the best beer selections in the U.S., Redlight, Redlight also now brews its own beer.

centralfloridaaletrail.com

TIP
If you can't decide what brewery to visit, book a guided bus tour of area breweries with Hop On! Brew Tours.

CHECK OUT THESE BREWERIES

Orlando Brewing, Orlando
orlandobrewing.com

Central 28 Beer Company, DeBary
central28beer.com

Ten10 Brewing Company, Orlando
ten10brewingcompany.com

Red Cypress Brewery, Winter Springs
redcypressbrewery.com

Hourglass Brewing, Longwood
hourglassbrewing.com

Broken Cauldron Taproom, Orlando
brokencauldrontaproom.com

Ivanhoe Park Brewing Company, Orlando
ivanhoeparkbrewing.com

Sanford Brewing Company, Sanford
sanfordbrewing.com

Crooked Can Brewery, Winter Garden
crookedcan.com

Persimmon Hallow Brewing Company, DeLand
persimmonhollowbrewing.com

COOK YOUR OWN PANCAKES
AT DE LEON SPRINGS

There is nothing in the world like getting the family together, heading to a state park, and making pancakes to get your day started. If that sounds amazing, then De Leon Springs is the park, and the Old Spanish Sugar Mill Restaurant is the restaurant. Every table has its own griddle, and the servers bring you homemade pancake batter so you can make them right there with your family. You can also add berries, chocolate chips, and other ingredients to customize your pancakes.

After you've stuffed your stomach, walk the park. Records show that Native Americans lived around the Springs at least six thousand years ago. In the 1800s, it became a winter resort because people up north were told that the Springs were actually a fountain of youth. Visit the Springs to take in this fascinating history lesson.

601 Ponce de Leon Blvd.
De Leon Springs, FL 32130
(386) 985-5644
floridastateparks.org/deleonsprings

TIP

If you have a party of 10 or more, consider making a reservation because space it limited.

BONUS TIP

The Old Spanish Sugar Mill also serves vegan and gluten-free pancakes.

GO VEG
IN CENTRAL FLORIDA

Believe it or not, Central Florida is one the best spots in the US to be a vegetarian or vegan. Restaurants that cater to plant-based eaters include Ethos Vegan Kitchen, Dixie Dharma at Market on South, The Sanctum, Dandelion Communitea Café, Veggie Garden, and Woodlands. Every October Orlando hosts the annual Central Florida Veg Fest, one of the largest and longest-running vegan festivals in the world. (No animals were harmed in the writing of this "Thing to Do.")

TIP
If you have a vegan sweet tooth, try Erin McKenna's Bakery NYC at Disney Springs. The bakery makes gluten free, vegan and kosher desserts.

Ethos Vegan Kitchen, Winter Park
ethosvegankitchen.com

Dixie Dharma at Market on South, Orlando
dixiedharma.com

The Sanctum, Orlando
thesanctumcafe.com

Dandelion Communitea Café, Orlando
dandelioncommunitea.com

Veggie Garden, Orlando
veggiegardenfl.com

Woodlands, Orlando
woodlandsusa.com

CELEBRATE CHRISTMAS YEAR-ROUND
AT FROSTY'S CHRISTMASTIME LOUNGE

Christmas is the most wonderful time of the year, so why do we only celebrate it in December? Not so at Frosty's Christmastime Lounge in downtown Orlando. This Saint Nicholas–inspired watering hole celebrates the season year-round. Decorated with reindeer, Santa Claus displays, and a Lionel train set, Frosty's Christmastime Lounge is a merry place that even the Scrooge in your group will enjoy. Watch holiday movies while sipping alcohol-infused craft snow cones, the bar's specialty. If you're there long enough, you'll see snow falling from the ceiling. The only thing missing is a roaring fire with chestnuts. (It's simply too hot in Florida to have that, right?) Merry Christmas!

50 E. Central Blvd.
Orlando, FL 32801
(407) 969-0911
frostys-orlando.com

EAT OYSTERS
AT LEE & RICK'S OYSTER BAR

If you pull up to a building that looks like a ship, you're in the right place. Lee & Rick's Oyster Bar is an Orlando institution that's been feeding seafood lovers for more than sixty-five years. It started as a nine-stool establishment that served *only* oysters. It has since expanded the building and menu, but oysters are still the main attraction. Order a bucket (raw, of course) and watch the staff at Lee & Rick's shuck them right in front of you. This no-frills restaurant should be a required stop for anyone who truly loves Orlando.

5621 Old Winter Garden Rd.
Orlando, FL 32811
(407) 293-3587
leeandricksoysterbar.com

BECOME A CHOCOLATIER
AT PETERBROOKE CHOCOLATIER
OF WINTER PARK

No, it's not Willy Wonka, but Peterbrooke Chocolatier of Winter Park is as close as you're going to get in Central Florida. A real-life chocolatier will show you how the chocolate is made and then give you samples. You can even throw a private party at Peterbrooke for a group of friends, where the whole gang puts on aprons, hats, and gloves and learns the chocolate making, and eating, process. You can even bring along a bottle of wine or champagne to celebrate after the tasting is over.

300 S. Park Ave.
Winter Park, FL 32789
(407) 644-3200
peterbrookewp.com

TIP
Peterbrooke Chocolatier of Winter Park actually has a summer camp for children, where they learn the ins and outs of the chocolate business.

MORE SWEET SPOTS IN ORLANDO

Angell and Phelps, Daytona Beach
angellandphelps.com

Chocolate Kingdom, Kissimmee
chocolatekingdom.com

Farris and Foster's Famous Chocolate Factory, Orlando
farrisandfosters.com

The Glass Knife, Winter Park
theglassknife.com

EAT A DAY'S WORTH OF CALORIES
AT DONUT KING

Anyone who has lived in Central Florida for even a short amount of time will recognize Donut King's yellow and blue box. If you spot it at your office or family event, you know someone cares about quality. This Minneola bakery and restaurant makes its doughnuts in house, fresh every day. What makes them so special? Well, you just have to go and try one. Donut King is open twenty-four hours a day, seven days a week. If Minneola is too far to drive, Donut King also has a location in Winter Park.

208 S. Hwy. 27
Minneola, FL 34715
(352) 243-4046

3716 Howell Branch Rd.
Winter Park, FL 32792
(321) 316-4817

thedonutking.com

OTHER GREAT SPOTS FOR DOUGHNUTS

Voodoo Doughnuts, Orlando
voodoodoughnut.com

Little Blue Donut Co., Winter Park
littlebluedonut.com

Valkyrie Doughnuts, Orlando
valkyriedoughnuts.com

GET SAUCED
AT THE BEST BBQ IN TOWN

The South is known for its barbecue, and Central Florida has some killer spots. One of the most popular is 4 Rivers Smokehouse. While the original location in Winter Park is now a taco restaurant, the new location down the street is just as busy as ever. Owner John Rivers has expanded his barbecue empire across the region, including locations in Gainesville, Tampa, Coral Springs, and Atlanta.

Everything on the menu at 4 Rivers Smokehouse is amazing, but if you can only try one item, get the 4 Rivers Signature Brisket. Trust us!

Multiple locations
4rsmokehouse.com

TIP
If you get a chance to hear owner John Rivers speak about how he stumbled into the restaurant business, it's worth an hour to hear his story.

OTHER LOCAL BBQ GREATS

Bubbalou's Bodacious Bar-B-Que, many locations
bubbalous.com

Caro-Bama, Orlando
caro-bamabbq.com

Firehouse BBQ
firehousebbq.us

Sugarboo's Bar-B-Q, Mount Dora
sugarboo.com

Porkie's Original BBQ, Apopka
porkiesapopka.com

EAT A *HUGE* SUNDAE
AT ALLEN'S CREAMERY & COFFEEHOUSE IN WINDERMERE

You might want to wear the loose-fitting pants for this one. Allen's Creamery & Coffeehouse in downtown Windermere—about ten miles west of Orlando—has one of the most unique food challenges in Central Florida. The Allen's Chain of Lakes Challenge pits you against eleven scoops of ice cream (one for each of the eleven lakes around Windermere), six toppings of your choice, and a mound of whipped cream, with, of course, a cherry on top. The brave souls willing to take up this challenge have fifteen minutes to finish the entire bowl of ice cream. If you do, you get a T-shirt! For those who just want a scoop of ice cream, Allen's Creamery has regular portions too.

523 Main St.
Windermere, FL 34786
(407) 876-3558
allenscreamery.com

CATCH DINNER AND A MOVIE...
AT THE SAME TIME

Date night has never been this cool! The Enzian lets you have dinner and a movie (and drinks) all in one place. Located in Maitland, the theater showcases some of the best independent movies, along with other classics, in an environment second to none: comfy chairs, your own table, and servers! If you're looking to see a film that's perhaps a bit more obscure in a setting that doesn't feel like a megaplex, the Enzian is your place.

1300 S. Orlando Ave.
Maitland, FL 32751
(407) 629-0054
enzian.org

TIP
As with many attractions in Orlando, plan ahead. If you want a good table, be there at least thirty minutes early.

MUSIC AND ENTERTAINMENT

TAKE A HIDDEN TOUR
OF WALT DISNEY WORLD

If you have lived in Orlando for any length of time, you have probably "done Disney" several times by now. How about taking it up a notch and getting a "secret tour"? For an extra $99 on top of general admission (price at publication), you get a five-hour tour of areas most people will never visit.

During the "Keys to the Kingdom" tour, you get to see the "utilidors," the famous underground tunnels that cast members use to get around the park. You will also learn about hidden messages and secret signs scattered throughout the park. You get to ride two rides during the tour while learning the secrets behind each one. When you are done, you will know things about Walt Disney and Mickey Mouse that even the most die-hard Disney fans don't know.

disneyworld.disney.go.com/events-tours/magic-kingdom/
keys-to-the-kingdom-tour

To book reservations, call (407) WDW-TOUR or (407) 939-8687.

TIP
Leave the cameras in the locker. No pictures are allowed on your behind-the-scenes tour.

EXPLORE SOMEWHERE,
BEYOND THE SEA (WORLD)

SeaWorld Orlando is one of the most popular theme parks in Central Florida. (Okay, you already knew that.) You can get up close and personal with animals from all over the world, including the penguins in the Antarctica: Empire of the Penguin exhibit. If you enjoy roller-coasters, SeaWorld Orlando has recently added Mako, the tallest, fastest, and longest coaster in Central Florida.

But if you haven't swum with the dolphins at Discovery Cove, then you're not quite a SeaWorld guru yet.

Discovery Cove is an all-inclusive park that allows you to swim with the dolphins and snorkel with an array of sea creatures in the Grand Reef. When you've had enough of the wildlife, you can slow it down with a casual float down a pristine lazy river or relax in a sunken terrace and enjoy a cold beverage. On those hot summer days in Orlando when you can't think of something cool to do, this may be one of the coolest ideas in town.

6000 Discovery Cove Way
Orlando, FL 32821
(407) 513-4600
discoverycove.com

TIP
Reservations are required. The park only lets in around 1,300 people per day, so you need to book at least a month out.

PLAY A MEAN PINBALL
AT THE PINBALL LOUNGE

Where in Central Florida can you play a "mean pinball"? At the Pinball Lounge, of course. Located inside the Oviedo Bowling Center about twenty-five miles northeast of Orlando, the Pinball Lounge features the largest concentration of pinball machines in Central Florida. Pinball fanatics and lifelong collectors of pinball machines Kurt van Zyl and Ed Klamp opened the retro arcade in 2014, and it has since become a destination. The lounge now boasts more than twenty machines, with some dating back to the 1960s. There's also a bar attached to the Pinball Lounge if you happen to get thirsty while hitting those flippers.

376 E. Broadway St.
Oviedo, FL 32765
(407) 495-2875
thepinballlounge.com

TIP
One of the best days to visit is Friday, when the Pinball Lounge hosts "Flip-Out Fridays" and it's unlimited play from 8:00 p.m. to midnight for only $10.

OTHER SPOTS TO PLAY OLD ARCADE GAMES

Player 1, Orlando
player1orlando.com

Joysticks, Orlando
joysticksorlando.com

VISIT A NEW THEME PARK
IN AN OLD LOCATION

While LEGOLAND Florida is one of the newest theme parks in Central Florida, the site where it's located in Polk County has a long history. The park is located in what used to be known as Cypress Gardens, which was actually one of Florida's original theme parks. The park became famous for daredevil water skiers and exotic backdrops, such as the Banyan tree planted in 1939 that is now the size of a city block. Thankfully when LEGOLAND took over the park in 2011 it kept Cypress Gardens in pristine shape. This area is how people around the world "viewed" Florida in the 1950s and '60s, with such stars as Elvis Presley and Johnny Carson making trips to the park. Such movies as *Easy to Love* and *Moon over Miami* were at least partially filmed on location.

The park is geared toward children twelve and younger, but there's plenty of fun for adults too. Miniland features some of the world's most famous buildings in LEGO form. There is also a water-ski show performed by LEGO characters, and it's worth strolling through the botanical gardens.

1 Legoland Way
Winter Haven, FL 33884
(888) 690-5346
florida.legoland.com

TIP
Before you go, get a sense for the park's history by watching online movies such as *Cypress Gardens: 70 Years of Magic.*

WATCH A ROCKET LAUNCH
ON THE BEACH

When rockets launch from the Kennedy Space Center, you can usually see them, or at least hear them, from most places in Central Florida. It's one thing to see the launch from a distance, but to get the full experience you need to get as close to Cape Canaveral as possible. In recent years, Space X, the company owned by billionaire Elon Musk, has been testing and launching rockets from Cape Canaveral. If you can time it right or live in Central Florida, seeing a rocket launch is a must-do event.

TIP
One of the best spots to watch a rocket launch is in (or near) the water. The waters of the Intracoastal Waterway or along the beach with your toes in the sand make for an unforgettable experience.

WATCH DISAPPEARING ISLAND APPEAR

One of the most popular beaches in all of Central Florida is a stretch of sand that is actually *not* always there. It's called Disappearing Island. When it's there, just head to the Intracoastal Waterway on the northern edge of New Smyrna Beach, just south of Ponce Inlet, to find out what the buzz is all about.

When the tide is out for the day, an island with soft sand appears where you can hang out and soak up the sun before the next high tide. On some days, hundreds of boaters flock to the island and park their boats right on the shore. Some people snorkel, some barbecue, some play corn toss, and others just enjoy the sandbar you can reach only by boat.

TIP
Be careful if you beach your boat and the tide is not fully out! You may be stuck until the tide comes back in.

BONUS TIP
On the western side of Disappearing Island is a canal that can protect boats from the waves.

GET UP CLOSE AND PERSONAL
WITH SNAKES

Even if you're afraid of snakes, a trip to Reptile World Serpentarium in St. Cloud may be a good thing. Why? Because of owner and snake handler George Van Horn, who knows a lot about snakes and why they shouldn't be feared. Open since 1972, Reptile World features more than eighty species of venomous and nonvenomous snakes. Twice a day, at noon and 3:00 p.m., Van Horn performs "Venom Extraction Shows," and you get to watch. If snakes really, really aren't your thing, though, Reptile World is also home to birds, alligators, turtles, and bearded dragons.

5705 E. Irlo Bronson Hwy.
St. Cloud, FL 34771
(407) 892-6905
reptileworldserpentarium.com

LAUGH, LAUGH, LAUGH
WITH THE FOLKS AT SAK COMEDY LAB

Sak Comedy Lab in downtown Orlando is improv at its best. Since 1991, the team of actors at Sak Comedy Lab has made audiences laugh by taking suggestions and making up characters and scenes on the spot. It's a lot like *Whose Line Is it Anyway?*, only Drew Carey probably won't be hosting. Several shows can be seen on weekend nights (early shows are geared toward families) at the 250-seat venue, and, if you like what you see on stage, Sak Comedy Lab also offers improv classes.

29 S. Orange Ave.
Orlando, FL 32801
(407) 648-0001
sak.com

TIP
You can find many open-mic comedy nights around Central Florida, including at Austin's Coffee in Winter Park and the Drunken Monkey in Orlando.

GET COLORING AND MORE
AT THE CRAYOLA EXPERIENCE

If you thought coloring was just a rainy-day activity, then you've never been to the Crayola Experience at the Florida Mall. This 70,000-square-foot attraction is Central Florida's most "colorful" experience. The hands-on attraction features more than twenty-five activities for children aged zero to a hundred. (Adults love coloring, too, right?) The Crayola Experience is more than just coloring. Learn how crayons are made, make your own melted-wax artwork, star in your own coloring page, and try out a 4-D coloring adventure. Plan to spend three to four hours at the Crayola Experience.

8001 S. Orange Blossom Trail
Orlando, FL 32809
(407) 757-1700
crayolaexperience.com/orlando

LOVE THE BLUES
AT BLUE MAN GROUP

This show is just flat-out fun! Take the children, the in-laws, the outlaws, or go by yourself! It really doesn't matter. You just need to go. You may be familiar with the Blue Man Group's act, but until you see it in person, you have no idea how talented these guys are or how hard you can laugh in one night. This is the type of show you can see more than once and still enjoy it every time.

Blue Man Theatre
CityWalk @ Universal Orlando
Orlando, FL 32819
(407) 258-3626
blueman.com

TIP
Make a night of it. Plan to grab dinner at one of the many restaurants at Universal City Walk, catch the show, and then spend the evening back on City Walk.

BONUS TIP
Stick around in the lobby after the show. The men in blue start wandering around a few minutes after the performance is over to meet the audience. Be sure to take your photo with the Blue Men and their live band.

WALK THE BOARDWALK
IN DAYTONA BEACH

The World's Most Famous Beach is still one of the most fun places around. The Daytona Beach Boardwalk and Pier has been spruced up lately. So if it's been a few years since you've been there, you owe it to yourself to check it out again. From the Ferris wheel to the fun shops and the bandshell, this takes you back in time to the way you remember beach boardwalks from the movies. New restaurants on the pier make this a fun beach getaway for a day.

Daytona Beach Boardwalk and Pier
Daytona Beach, FL 32118
daytonabeachboardwalk.com

TIP
All summer long on Saturday nights you can see fireworks on Daytona Beach at 9:45.

SEE CENTRAL FLORIDA
FROM A SEAPLANE

The Orlando area has hundreds of lakes, and so it only makes sense that Tavares is "America's Seaplane City. It's pretty common to see the seaplanes in the skies over Central Florida these days, but did you know that you can actually take a flight in a seaplane from downtown Tavares? Jones Brothers and Co. offers flightseeing tours that show off a totally unique view of Central Florida.

150 E. Ruby St.
Tavares, FL 32778
(352) 508-1800
jonesairandsea.com

TIP
It's not as expensive as you might think, with two-person packages starting at around $50 per person. Rides typically last between 20 and 30 minutes. If you want a longer ride, that could be worked out as well.

LISTEN TO TUNES
AT TIMUCUA WHITE HOUSE

When you pull up to the Timucua White House in Orlando for the first time, you're going to think: Am I at the right place? If it looks like a big white house in a residential neighborhood, the answer is yes. This music and arts venue, which is run by the Timucua Arts Foundation, doubles as someone's home, hosting more than seventy events a year. Expect to hear jazz, classical, alternative rock, and world music. The venue also hosts live theater. Most performances ask for a suggested donation of $10 to $20. Also, it's customary to bring a bottle of wine or food to share with other guests.

2000 S. Summerlin
Orlando, FL 32806
(321) 234-3985
timucua.com

OTHER SPOTS TO HEAR LIVE JAZZ MUSIC

Blue Bamboo Center for the Arts, Winter Park
bluebambooartcenter.com

Heidi's Jazz Club, Cocoa Beach
heidisjazzclub.com

Jazz Tastings, Maitland
jazztastings.com

SEE LIVE THEATER
AT THE ORLANDO SHAKES

To be or not to be, that is the question, and here's another question: Did you know Orlando has a theater that specializes in the works of Shakespeare? Orlando Shakes (formerly called the Orlando Shakespeare Theatre) in Loch Haven Park has been performing the works of the great English playwright since 1989. If Shakespeare doesn't interest you, though, don't fret; the theater also produces other classic, contemporary, and children's plays. Productions run throughout the year, so it's best to check the Orlando Shakes website for the latest information on performances.

812 E. Rollins St.
Orlando, FL 32803
(407) 447-1700
orlandoshakes.org

OTHER APPLAUSE-WORTHY THEATERS

Orlando Repertory Theatre, Orlando
orlandorep.com

Mad Cow Theatre, Orlando
madcowtheatre.com

Garden Theatre, Winter Garden
gardentheatre.org

Bay Street Players, Eustis
baystreetplayers.org

Winter Park Playhouse, Winter Park
winterparkplayhouse.org

Sonnentag Theatre at the IceHouse, Mount Dora
icehousetheatre.com

Orlando Fringe Theatre Festival, Orlando
orlandofringe.org

STRIKE OUT
FOR SOME UPSCALE BOWLING

Bowling has come a long way in recent years. The smoke-filled alleys of yesteryear are mostly extinct. Now, bowling is an upscale experience with great dining options too. Kings Dining and Entertainment, an upscale bowling alley in Orlando, is a great night out for adults, complete with some of the most exotic drinks in town. You can even get fresh seafood and steaks, which is light years ahead of the hot dogs and nachos you probably ate at the alley as a teenager. As a matter of fact, unlike at many bowling alleys, all the food here is made from scratch.

At Splitsville Luxury Lanes, you can even get sushi and margaritas while you roll a few games. This alley is at Disney Springs, so if you need to duck away and unwind for a couple of hours, this may be the place for you.

Kings Dining and Entertainment Orlando
8255 International Dr.
Orlando, FL 32819
(407) 363-0200
kings-de.com

Splitsville Luxury Lanes
1494 E. Buena Vista Dr.
Lake Buena Vista, FL 32830
(407) 938-7467
splitsvillelanes.com

RIDE THE WORLD'S TALLEST SWING
AT THE ORLANDO STARFLYER

For one of the best and most thrilling views of Central Florida, there may be no better attraction than the Orlando StarFlyer. At 450 feet, the attraction on International Drive is the world's tallest set of swings. If you're afraid of heights, this probably isn't the attraction for you. For everyone else, the Orlando StarFlyer is something you just shouldn't miss. The "Swings on Steroids" take riders straight up nearly 450 feet while swinging them around 360 degrees at 45 miles per hour. Is it windy up there? You better believe it. The entire ride lasts about four minutes and will be something you can brag about for the rest of your life.

8375 International Dr.
Orlando, FL 32819
(321) 888-2690
iconorlando.com

TIP
If you ride the Orlando StarFlyer, be sure to also check out all the other attractions at ICON Orlando 360, including ICON Orlando (formerly the Orlando EYE), Madame Tussauds Orlando, SEA LIFE Orlando Aquarium, SKELETONS: Museum of Osteology, and Arcade City.

SOLVE PUZZLES AND ESCAPE
FROM THE ESCAPE GAME ORLANDO

Your mission, if you choose to accept it, is to solve mind-teasers, riddles, math problems, and word games to get out of a locked room. You have sixty minutes, and time starts . . . now! That's basically the concept of The Escape Game Orlando and most other escape rooms in Central Florida. This family-friendly, live adventure requires teamwork, brain power, and quick thinking. The Escape Game Orlando features five themed games, including one set on the planet Mars and another set in a 1950s prison.

8145 International Dr., #511
Orlando, FL 32819
(407) 501-7222
orlandoescapegame.com

TIP
It's best to take a team with you to any escape room. When racing against the clock, the more brains working the problems, the better.

ESCAPE FOR A DAY
TO WEKIVA ISLAND

Many people who live in Central Florida swear they will never swim in the lakes and rivers (for obvious reasons). So if you have always wanted to splash around in the crystal-clear spring waters but were afraid to try, Wekiva Island in Longwood is the place to check that off your list. This "island" dates back decades but is under new ownership, and it's better than ever before. The boardwalk that runs the length of the stream on the island is a perfect spot to lounge in the sun or jump into the seventy-two-degree waters of the Wekiva River. The island has sand volleyball courts and plenty of room for the children to run, as well. Plus, it has many places to grab an "adult" beverage and listen to music on the water's edge. This is a complete day trip just a few miles from I-4.

1014 Miami Springs Dr.
Longwood, FL 32779
(407) 862-1500
wekivaisland.com

TIP
Rent a canopy for the day. It's a place to get away from the sun and claim a comfy chair right next to the beautiful stream.

BONUS TIP
Rent a canoe and paddle toward the Wekiva Springs. The odds are good that you will see some pretty hefty gators away from all the activity of the island fun.

HEAR MUSIC
AT THE PARKING LOT BLUEGRASS JAM IN OCOEE

Every Friday night for more than twenty-five years, a dedicated band of bluegrass musicians has gathered in a parking lot in Ocoee to jam, share stories, and continue the tradition of mountain music. The open jam at the corner of Maguire Road and State Road 50 in the parking lot of the Twistee Treat welcomes pickers, fiddlers, and singers of all ages and skill levels. Sometimes up to sixty or seventy spectators—from all corners of the globe—gather to listen to the music. There's a small-town charm about this event that every Central Floridian should experience at least once.

Twistee Treat of Ocoee
1500 Maguire Rd.
Ocoee, FL 34761

TIP
If you plan on attending the Parking Lot Bluegrass Jam in Ocoee, be sure to bring a lawn chair. There's no seating in the parking lot.

GO UP, UP, AND AWAY
IN A HOT AIR BALLOON

There is really no way to describe the feeling of floating on air with a bird's-eye view of Orlando and its attractions. These hot air balloon rides (typically one hour) take you over our Central Florida paradise, where you can truly see it all but hear practically no noise at all. Tours start early as the sun rises over the coast and before the daily storms start to brew. After certain flights, you also get champagne and breakfast.

Orlando Balloon Rides
44294 US Hwy. 27
Davenport, FL 33897
(407) 894-5040
orlandoballoonrides.com

Aerostat Adventures
2775 Florida Plaza Blvd.
Kissimmee, FL 34746
(407) 476-7101
hotairballoonorlando.com

TIP
Bring a jacket. It can be cool on those early morning rides in the sky!

GET BACK TO NATURE
ON THE LAKE APOPKA WILDLIFE DRIVE

Seeing nature is one of the great benefits of living in or visiting Florida, but sometimes it's just so gosh darn hot outside. For those who want to experience the beauty of nature from an air-conditioned car, the Lake Apopka Wildlife Drive is just for you. This one-way, eleven-mile drive hugs the north shore of Lake Apopka, which, at 48.4 square miles, is the fourth largest lake in Florida. During the drive, you will likely see birds, mammals, and some of the largest alligators in the region. Several "pull over" areas provide visitors a chance to stop along the drive. The Lake Apopka Wildlife Drive is open Fridays, Saturdays, and Sundays between sunrise and sunset.

Lake Apopka Wildlife Drive
2850 Lust Rd.
Apopka, FL 32703
(386) 329-4404
sjrwmd.com/lands/recreation/lake-apopka/wildlife-drive

Orlando Wetlands Park
25155 Wheeler Rd.
Christmas, FL 32709
(407) 568-1706
cityoforlando.net/wetlands

TIP
The Orlando Wetlands Park in east Orange County is another great place to see lots of alligators and birds.

SPORTS AND RECREATION

WATCH THE SEA COWS
AT BLUE SPRING

When the days get cool but the water stays warm, Blue Spring State Park in Volusia County becomes manatee heaven. This seventy-three-degree spring is a designated manatee refuge for the West Indian manatees, and they come here in bunches. If it's a cool morning, you might see several hundred of the sea cows swimming gracefully through the waters.

You can also walk the trails and take a cruise along the St. Johns River. If you are a scuba diver, you can take part in a cave dive in the spring, going down several hundred feet.

2100 W. French Ave.
Orange City, FL 32713
(386) 775-3663

Blue Springs
floridastateparks.org/bluespring

St. Johns River Cruises
sjrivercruises.com

TIP
If you plan to visit the park during holidays or the weekend, get there early because the park closes early once it reaches capacity.

GO BACK IN TIME
ON THE DORA CANAL

The Dora Canal has been called "the most beautiful mile of water in the world," and for good reason. The canal connects Lake Dora and Lake Eustis in Lake County. It is lined with 2,000-year-old cypress trees and wildlife galore. If you take off from the docks in Mt. Dora, you get a lakeside view of Mt. Dora, Eustis, and the county seat of Tavares. You also get a unique perspective of the beautiful homes along the golf course on Deer Island.

Premier Boat Tours
doracanaltour.com

Lake County boat tours
lakecountyfl.gov/boating/guided_tours.aspx

Lakeside Inn
lakeside-inn.com

TIP
You can also tour the canal by kayak, but you have to be brave. The twelve-foot gators are right at eye level!

VISIT ONE OF THE HIGHEST POINTS
IN CENTRAL FLORIDA

Here's a secret that even many locals may not know about: the Citrus Tower in Clermont. The Orlando area first developed as an agricultural hub because of the citrus industry, and this tower lets you see how it all happened. On a clear day, you can see eight counties from the observation deck of this 226-foot tower in southern Lake County. You can even see downtown Orlando and Walt Disney World when the skies are blue! It's a view of Florida you can only get from that high above the earth.

141 US 27
Clermont, FL 34711
(352) 394-4061
citrustower.com

TIP
For an added treat, head to the Citrus Tower during the Christmas holiday. The tower is lit up like a twenty-two-story Christmas tree with a light display set to music.

PADDLEBOARD
ALONG TURNER FLATS

Paddleboarding may look like hard work, but it's really not as tough as you think. There are numerous places to paddleboard along the coast and on the lakes in Central Florida, but if you want to see some of the most pristine areas in the state from the water, you need to find a place near the Canaveral National Seashore. One of the best spots is along Turner Flats, north of the national park near JB's Fish Camp in New Smyrna Beach. Most days you can see manatees, dolphins, exotic birds, and thousand-year-old trees. The water is often very calm, so it will take only a few minutes to conquer the paddleboard without being hit by a rogue wave.

Paddleboard rentals near the Canaveral National Seashore

East Coast Paddle, New Smyrna Beach
eastcoastpaddle.com

JB's Fish Camp, New Smyrna Beach
jbsfishcamp.com

Paddling Paradise, Palm Bay
paddlingparadise.com

TIP
When paddling the area near the Canaveral National Seashore, wear water shoes. Oyster shells can slice up your feet.

CHEER ON ORLANDO'S SPORTS TEAMS

Orlando may not have an MLB, NFL, or NHL team, but we still love sports, and we show our pride by supporting our teams . . . even when they aren't doing so great.

The Orlando Magic played its inaugural season in 1989, and we've been basketball fans ever since. During the NBA season, be sure to catch a game at the Amway Center, one of the best sports venues in the United States. The Amway Center is also home to Orlando's professional hockey team, the Orlando Solar Bears.

Just down the street is where the Orlando City Lions and Orlando City Pride play their home games. The men's (Lions) and women's (Pride) teams draw thousands of purple-clad fans on game days. If you've never experienced a live soccer game, be sure to snag a few tickets to a game.

Like the rest of Florida, Orlando loves football. Orlando's Camping World Stadium hosts a preseason NFL game every few years, and the NFL Pro Bowl has been played at the stadium since 2017. The University of Central Florida Knights play their home games at Spectrum Stadium, located on the UCF campus about twenty miles east of downtown Orlando. In recent years, the UCF Knights have stunned the college football world by winning both the Fiesta Bowl and the Peach Bowl.

Orlando Magic
Amway Center, 400 W. Church St.
Orlando, FL 32801

Orlando City Soccer
Orlando City Stadium, 655 W. Church St.
Orlando, FL 32805

Camping World Stadium
1 Citrus Bowl Place
Orlando, FL 32805

UCF Knights
Spectrum Stadium, 4465 Knights Victory Way
Orlando, FL 32816

TIP
Parking can be tricky for some of the downtown Orlando sporting events. If possible, try taking SunRail or using a ride-sharing app to get a lift to the game.

JUST DO FUN SPOT AMERICA ALREADY!

You see the commercials, you drive by the parks in Orlando and Kissimmee, and it always looks like a lot of fun. Here's a news flash . . . it is fun! The Fun Spot America location in Orlando near International Drive has two roller-coasters: White Lightning, a wooden roller-coaster, and Freedom Flyer, an inverted steel coaster that's been recently upgraded with a virtual reality experience.

At the Kissimmee location, the Mine Blower coaster is the only wooden coaster in Florida to go upside down, and the Rockstar coaster whips you around as it goes around sharp corners.

Both locations have many other rides and attractions to keep you and the children happy.

And, yes, it's HUGE!!!! (Locals will get that.)

5700 Fun Spot Way
Orlando, FL 32819
(407) 363-3867

2850 Florida Plaza Blvd.
Kissimmee, FL 34746
(407) 363-3867
funspotattractions.com

TIP

Fun Spot America offers free parking, free admission, and rain checks. If it looks like a rainy Florida afternoon, your day (and your money) won't be lost.

PADDLE THE SWAN BOATS
AT LAKE EOLA

The swan boats are such an iconic part of downtown Orlando that some people never think twice about taking them for a spin, but the view from the middle of Lake Eola is unbelievable. Lake Eola is a beautiful urban water feature right in the middle of downtown and perfect for spending a day relaxing. The swan boats are very easy to paddle across the entire lake, where you can get up close and personal with some of the prized swans and other birds that call Lake Eola home.

512 E. Washington St.
Orlando, FL 32801
(407) 246-4484
cityoforlando.net/parks/lake-eola-park

TIP
For an added thrill, take the boats out at night. The city recently began allowing you to take them out when the sun goes down, which gives you a great view of the nighttime skyline and the fountain show.

BONUS TIP
Lake Eola Park is one of the most popular parks in all of Central Florida. Almost every weekend this downtown park hosts some kind of festival. Take a stroll after paddling.

FLOAT DOWN THE ROCK SPRINGS RUN
AT KELLY PARK

One of the best ways to cool off in the hot summer sun is a float down the crystal-clear waters at Kelly Park near Apopka. The sixty-eight-degree spring is just one part of Kelly Park but is certainly the reason swimmers flock here. You simply jump onto a tube and wind your way down the nearly one-mile Rock Springs Run and then do it again and again! It takes about twenty minutes to make the whole run, and then it's just a short walk back to the start. You can also enjoy many beaches in the area if you don't feel like chasing the children up paths.

400 E. Kelly Park Rd.
Apopka, FL 32712
(407) 254-1902

TIP
Be sure you get there early to get into the park. The park quickly fills up on hot summer days.

BONUS TIP
Bring along the snorkel gear.

SEE "LADY LIBERTY"
AT BIG TREE PARK

The Senator, one of the oldest trees in the world, had long been the centerpiece of Big Tree Park in Longwood, but an arsonist burned it to the ground in 2012. Thankfully, another tree called "Lady Liberty" is nearly as impressive. The bald cypress tree is approximately two thousand years old and is now the must-see tree in all of Central Florida. It's an easy walk to see the sights in the park, and thanks to renewed interest after the burning of the Senator, the park received some much-needed upgrades.

761 General Hutchison Pkwy.
Longwood, FL 32750
(407) 665-2001

TIP
This may not be an entire day trip for you, so bring the bikes or walking shoes. The park is also a trailhead for the Cross Seminole Trail.

GO BEHIND THE SCENES
AT THE DAYTONA INTERNATIONAL SPEEDWAY

There is nothing like feeling, hearing, seeing, and, yes, smelling a race at the Daytona International Speedway. If you have the chance to go to the Daytona 500, do it.

If you're not in the area during Race Week, however, the next best thing is a behind-the-scenes tour of the racetrack. The ninety-minute All Access Tour gives you a unique opportunity to explore the 2.5-mile Speedway. You'll get to visit the start/finish line and thirty-one-degree banks, and you'll ride down the pit road to get right next to the pit stalls. You'll also get to see the media deadline room and stand next to the car that won the most recent Daytona 500. (It may have some dents on it because the car is left in the same condition as the day it won the race.)

After the tour, you get access to the Motorsports Hall of Fame of America honoring all forms of motorsports: stock cars, sports cars, open-wheel, motorcycles, drag racing, land speed records, powerboating, and aviation.

1801 W. International Speedway Blvd.
Daytona Beach, FL 32114
(800) 748-7467
daytonainternationalspeedway.com

CELEBRATE AMERICA'S PASTIME
AT A SPRING TRAINING GAME

Baseball fans from cities up north flock to Central Florida every year to catch the first glimpse of baseball season, so it just makes sense that locals take part in this timeless ritual too. Even if you don't enjoy baseball, this is an experience that transcends the sport. It's a day of renewal when you know summer fun is right around the corner. The look on the children's faces when they see the green grass and catch a glimpse of their favorite players is priceless. The tickets are cheap, the level of play is fantastic, and it will certainly renew your sense of humanity. This is not just a game. This is a way of renewing your soul, even if it's just for one afternoon in the sun.

Teams currently playing in Central Florida:

Atlanta Braves, ESPN Wide World of Sports at Walt Disney World
mlb.com/braves

Detroit Tigers, Publix Field at Joker Marchant Stadium in Lakeland
mlb.com/tigers

TIP

Go ahead and splurge on the front-row seats. The players will likely talk to you, and the odds of getting a baseball souvenir are pretty good. If you miss Spring Training, go see a few minor league teams play in Kissimmee, Lakeland, or Daytona Beach.

SCALE AN INDOOR MOUNTAIN
AT AIGUILLE ROCK CLIMBING CENTER

Who says there are no mountains in Central Florida? At Aiguille Rock Climbing Center in Longwood, there's ten thousand square feet of climbing walls that reach heights of up to thirty-six feet. (OK, it's no Mount Everest, but it's a start.) The indoor climbing gym caters to thrill seekers ages four and up. Beginners get a course in climbing safety before heading up the climbing walls. You pay by the day ($16 plus rental fees for shoes, harness, and belay device), so feel free to take a break between climbs.

999 Charles St.
Longwood, FL 32750
(407) 332-1430
aiguille.com

TIP
If you don't like heights, Aiguille Rock Climbing Center also offers something called bouldering, which is rock climbing on smaller walls without the use of harnesses. There's even padding if you fall off.

SHOOT BIG GUNS
AT MACHINE GUN AMERICA

Machine Gun America may not be for everybody, but if you've ever wanted to shoot machine guns, pistols, or revolvers, this is your place. Machine Gun America calls itself "Orlando's first and only automatic adrenaline attraction." Everyone who shoots at Machine Gun America is provided with eye and ear protection, range targets, and one-on-one instructions from an armed, certified instructor. United States residents can experience Machine Gun America with a valid government-issued ID. International visitors should check with Machine Gun America before arriving at the attraction.

5825 W. Irlo Bronson Memorial Hwy.
Kissimmee, FL 34746
(407) 278-1800
machinegunamericaorlando.com

TIP
Machine Gun America also offers realistic simulation shooting experiences without live ammunition for those who don't want to shoot the real thing.

PUSH THE PEDAL TO THE METAL
AT ANDRETTI INDOOR KARTING AND GAMES

If you have the need for speed, race over to Andretti Indoor Karting and Games near International Drive. Here you can feel the adrenaline rush in state-of-the-art electric go-karts. These aren't the build-them-yourself go-karts you made in your garage as a teen. At Andretti Indoor Karting, you can go head-to-head against other racers around the climate-controlled indoor tracks filled with hairpin turns, elevation changes, and long straightaways. The entertainment complex also has arcade games, bowling, simulators, and laser tag.

9299 Universal Blvd.
Orlando, FL 32819
(407) 641-0415
andrettikarting.com

OTHER SPOTS TO GO GO-KARTING

Lil 500 Go-Kart Track, Maitland
lil500.com

Fun Spot America, Kissimmee and Orlando
fun-spot.com

I-Drive NASCAR Indoor Kart Racing, Orlando
idrivenascar.com

Orlando Kart Center
orlandokartcenter.com

SEE REAL LIVE COWBOYS
AT THE WESTGATE RIVER RANCH

The cattle business has deep roots in Central Florida, especially in Polk and Osceola counties, and there's nothing like a real live rodeo to remind you of the region's past. Every Saturday night at the Westgate River Ranch Resort, rodeo athletes compete in trick riding, barrel racing, and bull riding. The 1,200-seat arena sits on a nearly undisturbed 1,700-acre parcel of land overlooking the scenic Kissimmee River. If you happen to get inspired by the rodeo, there's a mechanical bull on the property for you to test your riding skills. Think you can last eight seconds?

3200 River Ranch Blvd.
River Ranch, FL 33867
(863) 692-1321
westgateresorts.com

TIP
If you plan accordingly, try to stay at the Westgate
River Ranch. Accommodations include hotel
rooms, tent sites, RV camping, and tipis.

TAKE FIDO OUT TO PLAY
AT A DOG PARK

Taking your pooch out for a walk is fun, but sometimes Fido may want to run around and be free. Central Florida is home to more than a dozen dog parks and dog-friendly beaches. The Lake Baldwin Dog Park is one of the largest—and most unique—dog parks in the region. Roughly twenty-three acres, Lake Baldwin Dog Park features a wooded area, open fields, and a sandy beach for your pup to play off leash. Over on the coast, dogs (on leash) are allowed at Smyrna Dunes Park in New Smyrna Beach. This seventy-three-arce park is situated on a peninsula. Get there early because parking is limited during peak times of the year.

Lake Baldwin Dog Park
2000 S. Lakemont Ave.
Winter Park, FL 32789
(407) 599-3334

Smyrna Dunes Park
2995 N. Peninsula Ave.
New Smyrna Beach, FL 32169
(386) 424-2935

ZIP THE CANYONS LIKE SUPERMAN
IN OCALA

So many ziplines can be found in Central Florida that it's hard to pick just one to put on your bucket list, but the Canyons Zip, billed as Florida's highest, longest, and fastest, has to be done. (By the way, you also do this zipline face-down "Superman style.") The Canyons Zip Line & Canopy Tours is a short drive north to Ocala, where miners abandoned limestone quarries nearly a hundred years ago. The area has been practically untouched since the work stopped in the 1930s. So this is a little bit adventure ride, history lesson, and nature tour. You'll reach speeds of up to fifty miles an hour flying across terrain that looks like it should be anywhere but Florida.

8045 NW Gainesville Rd.
Ocala, FL 34475
(352) 351-9477
zipthecanyons.com

TIP
For an added thrill, zip at night when the moon is full. You get to put on glow sticks and zip through the trees and see Florida in a way that few have seen before.

OTHER GREAT ZIPLINES IN THE ORLANDO AREA

Screamin' Gator at Gatorland, Orlando
gatorland.com

Treetop Trek Aerial Adventures, Melbourne
treetoptrek.com

Forever Florida, St. Cloud
foreverflorida.com/zip-line-adventures

Zoom Air at the Central Florida Zoo, Sanford
zoomair.us

Zoom Air at Tuscawilla Park, Daytona Beach
zoomair.us

GO SKYDIVING, INSIDE

For people who refuse to jump out of a perfectly good airplane at ten thousand feet, iFLY Orlando's indoor skydiving is the next best thing. It has all the thrills of a free fall without the expense of firing up the airplane. It will take you a few tries before you get it right, but once you've learned how to maneuver your body in the wind tunnel, it is quite a thrill. iFLY supplies all the gear you will need. If you're looking for a unique place for a birthday party or a get-together with friends, this is likely something they've never tried before.

8969 International Dr.
Orlando, FL 32819
(407) 337-4359
iflyworld.com/orlando

TIP
This is an activity where you get better very quickly. You could be a rookie today and doing high-flying stunts in a matter of weeks.

EXTRA POINT
You aren't being "blown up" by the fans. The fans are on the top and actually suck you toward the ceiling.

GO HANG GLIDING
IN "FLAT" KISSIMMEE

You may think you need a mountain or at least a cliff to hang glide, but that's not true. As a matter of fact, this specific type of hang gliding instruction was invented right here in Central Florida. It was invented at the Wallaby Ranch near Kissimmee, where you can still take part in a tandem hang gliding flight. You simply sit back and relax in the specially designed tandem (two-seat) glider on wheels while the airplane gently lifts you into the sky. It's called aerotowing, and it's very safe. Thrill seekers come from all over the world to try it out, so take advantage of this local attraction right in our own backyard.

1805 Deen Still Rd.
Davenport, FL 33897
(863) 424-0070
wallaby.com

TIP
You can camp on the property. The family can enjoy themselves in the swimming pool or on the playground while you take to the skies.

SEE MOUNT DORA
ON A SEGWAY

Walking is great, but sometimes in the Florida heat it can get exhausting. Also, who wouldn't want to see Mount Dora, one of Central Florida's most charming towns, while zipping along on a Segway? Central Florida Glides operates daily guided tours of the lakeside town. The one-hour adventure starts at the Segway of Central Florida dealership, where you'll get outfitted with a Segway and helmet. Before the tour, you'll also get a quick lesson on how to operate a Segway. The guides don't expect you to be an expert, and no experience is necessary to take the tour.

During the tour, you'll travel along the town's waterfront and city marina. You'll see the Mount Dora lighthouse, Palm Island Park, the town's historic neighborhood, and the Lakeside Inn.

430 N. Alexander St.
Mount Dora, FL 32757
(352) 383-9900
segwayofcentralflorida.com

GO SAILING IN SANFORD
ON LAKE MONROE

Port, starboard, keel, jib, windward, leeward, lines, heeling, helm
. . . do you know what these terms mean? If not, it's totally OK.
You may get to learn some of them while sailing on Lake Monroe
in Sanford. U-Sail of Central Florida, which operates out of the
Monroe Harbour Marina, offers sailing lessons for both visitors and
locals. Beginners may want to start with an "Introduction to Sailing"
class that includes two hours on the water with an instructor. You
can do as much as you like during the introductory class, or you can
just sit and let the wind blow through your hair. If you happen to
catch the sailing bug, U-Sail of Central Florida offers a variety of
more advanced classes.

A-Dock, 531 N. Palmetto Ave.
Sanford, FL 32771
(407) 330-0633
usailflorida.com

DO YOGA WITH A BABY GOAT
AT WILDFLOWER FARM IN ORLANDO

Baby. Goat. Yoga. Those three words typically don't go together, but baby goat yoga is really a thing, and it's just about as adorable as it sounds. Wildflower Farm, located in Orlando, is a working farm that offers outdoor yoga with baby goats, but, no, the goats don't do yoga. While you're doing your downward-facing dog or child's pose or side plank, baby goats scamper around the farm and will interact with you while you're on your mat. Can it be distracting? Yes. Is it fun? Oh, yeah. After class, plan on feeding the goats; they get hungry from all the attention. Baby goat yoga classes are offered only during select times of the year, so be sure to check the Wildflower Farm website.

2218 Carrington Dr.
Orlando, FL 32807
(407) 592-4103
wildflowerfarmorlando.com

TIP
Classes for Baby Goat Yoga fill up very quickly, so if you are interested, be sure to book ahead of time to get on the list.

GO SKIING
AT WINTERCLUB INDOOR SKI & SNOWBOARD IN WINTER PARK

Believe it or not, it did actually snow in Central Florida back in 1977, but that was pretty much the last time anyone saw real flurries in Orlando. Also, Central Florida isn't exactly home to any real mountains. So how can you go skiing here? WinterClub Indoor Ski & Snowboard in Winter Park allows you to feel the rush of going down a mountain without the cold, white flakes. WinterClub has two infinite slopes that resemble giant treadmills covered in white artificial turf. To create the effect of a downhill ski run, the turf moves uphill. For skiers and snowboarders, the smooth, moving surface is similar to snow. There's also a ski simulator that lets skiers and snowboarders experience the same G-force effects that they would on a real mountain.

2950 Aloma Ave.
Winter Park, FL 32792
(407) 618-1123
winterclubski.com

TIP
At WinterClub Indoor Ski & Snowboard, you can rent all the gear needed to experience the rush of downhill skiing or snowboarding.

RIDE THE
WEST ORANGE TRAIL

The state of Florida is progressing on paving a bike trail that will stretch from the Gulf Coast to the Atlantic Ocean. Thankfully for those of us in Central Florida, we already have many biking trails to explore until the cross-state trail is complete. If you want to experience the best trail rides the area has to offer, start in Winter Garden. You can begin at the Killarney Station near Lake Apopka, where you cross the restored railroad bridge. It's only about two miles to downtown Winter Garden, where the city has done an amazing job rehabbing its downtown. The bike trail goes right through the center of town, so you can see the shops and restaurants on both sides of you. That means you can ride a few miles and then grab some lunch. Then ride a few more miles and grab some ice cream. If you are feeling really adventurous, you can ride the entire twenty-two miles up to Apopka and then turn around and do it in reverse.

501 Crown Point Cross Rd.
Winter Garden, FL 34787
(407) 654-1108
orangecountyparks.net

OTHER GREAT TRAILS

Seminole Wekiva Trail
Park near Markham Woods Road to see the murals painted alongside the trail.

Little Econ Greenway
Park along Alafaya Trail near UCF. You get a great view of the Little Econ River, and there is even a butterfly garden along the way.

General James Van Fleet State Trail
It's a long trail with many paved miles for training, but it can be a bit lonely. It will eventually connect to all Central Florida trails.

PLAY GOLF WITH YOUR FEET
AT HAWK'S LANDING GOLF CLUB

Golf is hard and takes a lifetime to master. FootGolf is pretty simple: If you can kick a ball, you can play FootGolf. Combining soccer and golf, FootGolf is played with a soccer ball on an outdoor golf course. Players try to kick the ball into an oversized hole. The rules of FootGolf mimic the rules of regular golf, with the goal being to complete the course with the fewest number of strokes, or "kicks." Hawk's Landing Golf Club features an eighteen-hole course that's both fun and challenging for the entire family, and if you want to wear bright plaid pants while playing FootGolf, we won't stop you.

8701 World Center Dr.
Orlando, FL 32821
(800) 567-2623
golfhawkslanding.com/footgolf

TIP
FootGolf really is a sport the entire family can enjoy. It's not always all about kicking the ball really, really far. There's a lot of finesse that goes into FootGolf too.

OTHER FOOTGOLF COURSES

Disney's Oak Trail at Walt Disney World, Orlando
golfwdw.com/courses/disneys-oak-trail-golf-course

Sanctuary Ridge Golf Club, Clermont
sanctuaryridgecfl.com

Twin Rivers Golf Club, Oviedo
twinriversgolfclub.com

Remington Golf Club, Kissimmee
playgolfinremington.com

HOP ON THE LIMO CYCLE
IN SANFORD

This party is powered by your pedaling, so if you stop pedaling the party stops. Operating on the streets of historic downtown Sanford, the Limo Cycle is like a giant bicycle that's attached to a bar. Groups of up to fifteen people use the power of their legs to get the Limo Cycle around town during the two-hour tour. A trained driver steers you through the streets and takes you to Sanford's most popular bars, restaurants, and shops. While cruising around Sanford, don't be surprised if you get a few honks and waves from those who aren't on the Limo Cycle. Riders can bring along beer, cider, or wine, but all drinks must be consumed on the Limo Cycle. Riders under twenty-one years of age must be accompanied by a guardian.

303 W. Third St.
Sanford, FL 32771
(424) 299-4441
limocycle.com

TIP
You really do have to pedal on the Limo Cycle, so dress appropriately during Central Florida's hot summer months.

SEE ORLANDO BY BICYCLE
ON A JUICE BIKE

If you've lived in Orlando for any period of time, you know that traffic can be a nightmare, and don't even get us started on Interstate-4. While Lynx (the region's bus system) and SunRail (the region's commuter rail) are great, getting around by bicycle can be a blast. The best way to see Orlando by bicycle is by renting a Juice Bike. The bike-sharing company, known for its bright orange bikes, has more than thirty stations around Central Florida. You can reserve a bike online, on a mobile device, or at the docking station. Once it is reserved, you'll get a four-digit PIN to unlock the bike. All bikes are adjustable, so you tall riders don't have to worry. Rental rates start at $8 an hour. (A credit card is required.) When you're done riding, just lock it back up at any station or anywhere within the Juice Bike system for a $2 fee.

Juice Bike stations are located across Orlando.
(407) 930-9414
juicebikeshare.com

TIP
If you want to hop off the bike and grab a cup of coffee, you can use the lock that's provided to secure the bike to a nearby rack. When it's time to start riding again, you can enter a four-digit PIN to unlock the bike and go.

WRESTLE A GATOR
(SORT OF)

Gatorland is one of the original Florida attractions and still awesome—hundreds of gators spread out all across the alligator-themed park. You can even get up close and personal sitting on the back of a gator; you even get to hold its snout for pictures. The park has many attractions that will entertain people of all ages, but one of the highlights is certainly the Gator Wrestlin' Experience. You will also see exotic birds, Florida panthers, and some of the biggest snakes on the planet. The park even has a zipline tour that whizzes you right over the heads of the giant reptiles.

14501 S. Orange Blossom Trail
Orlando, FL 32837
(407) 855-5496
gatorland.com

TIP
Get to the wrestlin' show early to have your picture taken on the back of a gator. It's perfectly safe, and the children will show the picture to everyone they know.

OTHER GATOR-THEMED ATTRACTIONS

Reptile Discovery Center, DeLand
reptilediscoverycenter.com

Jungle Adventures Animal Park, Christmas
jungleadventures.com

CULTURE AND HISTORY

CLIMB TO THE MOON
AT PONCE INLET LIGHTHOUSE

The Ponce Inlet Lighthouse stands as a beacon in the small town of Ponce Inlet, just south of Wilbur by the Sea. It dates all the way back to 1887 and is still actively used as a navigational aid near the inlet's north shore. The tour of the tallest lighthouse in Florida (and the third tallest in the United States) is fun for the whole family. Visitors can also explore the grounds, which feature the lightkeepers' house, an oil storage building, a pump house, and a collection of lighthouse lenses.

You really need to be there for the rare event when the moon rises over the ocean and the sun sets on the horizon at the same time. The "Climb to the Moon" tour happens once a month and is open to only twenty-five people at a time, so plan ahead.

4931 S. Peninsula Dr.
Ponce Inlet, FL 32127
(386) 761-1821
ponceinlet.com

TIP

Don't get too fancy! Bring along your walking shoes to climb the steps of this 175-foot National Historic Landmark.

BONUS TIP

Another lighthouse to check out in Central Florida is at Cape Canaveral. canaverallight.org

SEE THE SHUTTLE ATLANTIS,
DINGS AND ALL

The days of seeing space shuttles launch from Cape Canaveral may be gone, but it's not too late to see a shuttle up close and personal. Inside the $100 million Kennedy Space Center Visitor Complex now sits the space shuttle Atlantis, the final orbiter to fly in space. They didn't even clean it up, either! You get to see Atlantis and the way it was after its final trip to space, dents and all. As cool as that is, you might be impressed by the giant screens near the ceiling that show how quickly the shuttle flew over the Earth. A video replication of a trip around the Earth shows the seven minutes it took for the shuttle to make one complete trip around the Earth.

SR 405
Kennedy Space Center, FL 32899
(855) 433-4210
kennedyspacecenter.com

TIP
Make time to do the Shuttle Launch Experience while you are there. You'll know why once you do.

TAKE A LEISURELY STROLL
AT LEU GARDENS

At certain times of the year, this may be the most beautiful place in all of Central Florida. Leu Gardens is a fifty-acre garden just minutes from downtown Orlando but feels like a world away. The gardens are home to thousands of native Florida plants and some of the most beautiful roses you've ever seen.

One of the most interesting parts of the tour is seeing inside the former home of Harry P. Leu and his wife, Mary Jane. The tour guides are excellent and give you more insight into how Leu helped develop Orlando into the metropolitan area it is today. If you're lucky, you may even stumble upon a wedding or one of the many concerts that are held on the grounds every year.

1920 N. Forest Ave.
Orlando, FL 32803
(407) 246-2620
leugardens.org

TIP
Take advantage of movie night, typically held on the first Friday night of the month. Picnic baskets and alcohol are allowed. Bring the bug spray too.

BONUS TIP
Leu Gardens hosts its annual plant sale every spring. If you plan on attending, bring a wagon to carry your plants.

GET ICE!
AT GAYLORD PALMS

Florida is known for its heat, but every holiday season "Ice! At Gaylord Palms" moves into town. This is a fantastic attraction that you have to see at least once and possibly once each year if you are lucky. Yes, it may be eighty degrees in December, but somehow the crew at the Gaylord Palms keeps this massive space at nine degrees Fahrenheit. The ice-carved characters are amazing, but wait until the end. The life-sized frozen nativity scene will likely be the crowd favorite for your group, as well. So if you have friends or family from up north in town for the holidays, this should definitely be on your list of things to do one afternoon to keep them happy.

6000 W. Osceola Pkwy.
Kissimmee, FL 34746
(407) 586-0000
gaylordpalms.com

TIP
Dress warmly! Gaylord Palms provides a parka, but you will want to dig out as many warm clothes as you can find, including gloves, boots, long underwear, and a hat.

BONUS TIP
Don't rush off after the tour.
Make time for the hot chocolate in the gift shop.

SEE GLOW-IN-THE-DARK SEA CREATURES

Water is not supposed to light up, but that's exactly what happens during nighttime bioluminescent kayak tours. In the warm lagoons of Mosquito Lagoon live billions of plankton called dinoflagellates that turn the water a bluish-white when disturbed. Best seen between June and early October, the plankton light up the dark waters with every paddle stroke or passing manatee, dolphin, or fish. You can even put your hand into the water and make it light up. One of the best tour companies to see the glow-in-the-dark creatures is A Day Away Kayak Tours. The nighttime tours start after sunset and typically last about ninety minutes.

Tours launch at the Merritt Island National Wildlife Refuge near Titusville.
(321) 268-2655
adayawaykayaktours.com

POLKA
AT WILLOW TREE

You don't have to be in Germany to enjoy Oktoberfest! Hollerbach's Willow Tree Café lets you schunkel with an oompah-pah band four nights a week right in the heart of historic downtown Sanford. Experience some gemuetlichkeit, which is that feeling of enjoying good food and drink among friends and family. You can order the brats, pretzels, and beer inside or on the patio at the restaurant rated as one of the top German beer halls in all of America.

205 E. First St.
Sanford, FL 32713
(407) 321-2204
willowtreecafe.com

TIP
If you plan on going on a weekend, you need to make a reservation about two weeks in advance, depending on the size of your entourage. Otherwise, you might be standing for an hour watching everyone else doing the polka.

INVESTIGATE NEW SMYRNA BEACH'S
MYSTERY RUINS

Two sets of ruins can be found in New Smyrna Beach. The history of one is known; the other is still a bit of a mystery. The story behind the Sugar Mill Ruins is well documented. It's a former mill that dates back to the nineteenth century. All that's left today are frames of these historic structures that were destroyed in the Seminole Indian War.

Not far away are more ruins, with a bit more mystery. They are known as the Turnbull Ruins. Nobody knows for sure what they were trying to build around 1776, but the foundation remains. Some think it was a fort, while others think it was supposed to be a mansion overlooking the Intracoastal Waterway. Whatever it was, it's worth a few minutes to explore for yourself.

Sugar Mill Ruins
1050 Old Mission Rd.
New Smyrna Beach, FL 32168
(386) 427-2284

Turnbull Ruins
115 Julia St.
New Smyrna Beach, FL 32168
(386) 424-2175

SEE TIFFANY GLASS
AT THE CHARLES HOSMER MORSE MUSEUM OF AMERICAN ART

The Morse Museum in downtown Winter Park has the world's most comprehensive collection of works by Louis Comfort Tiffany. Jewelry, pottery, paintings, art glass, leaded-glass lamps, and windows from the world-famous artist and designer fill the museum. One of the museum's most prized pieces is a Tiffany chapel from the 1893 World's Columbian Exposition in Chicago. The museum also features American art pottery, late nineteenth and early twentieth century American paintings, graphics, and decorative art.

445 N. Park Ave.
Winter Park, FL 32789
(407) 645-5311
morsemuseum.org

TIP
If you're in the area, stop at the Cornell Fine Arts Museum on the campus of Rollins College, which is free and has works of art ranging from antiquities to contemporary pieces.

OTHER CENTRAL FLORIDA ART MUSEUMS

Orlando Museum of Art, Orlando
omart.org

Mennello Museum of American Art, Orlando
mennellomuseum.org

Albin Polasek Museum & Sculpture Gardens, Winter Park
polasek.org

Cornell Fine Arts Museum, Winter Park
rollins.edu/cornell-fine-arts-museum

Museum of Art, DeLand
moartdeland.org

SEE WINTER PARK
FROM THE WATER

One of the most affluent cities in all of the United States is just a little bit north of Orlando, and many of the magnificent homes of Winter Park are hidden by heavily canopied tree-lined streets. So if you really want to see some of the most beautiful mansions in the state, you need to see them by boat. That's where the Winter Park Scenic Boat Tour comes into play. The tour takes you onto the Winter Park Chain of Lakes, where you learn all about the history of Winter Park. You cruise through lush canals, see Rollins College, and view the opulent homes of Winter Park residents.

312 E. Morse Blvd.
Winter Park, FL 32789
(407) 644-4056
scenicboattours.com

TIP
Make a day of it. Get to Winter Park early on a Saturday morning and browse around the Winter Park Farmers' Market. Then make a short drive or walk to Lake Osceola, where the boat tours begin. Follow that by grabbing lunch at any of the many sidewalk cafés in Winter Park.

FEEL THE RUMBLE
AT BIKE WEEK AND BIKETOBERFEST

It's such a tradition that you might overlook this world-famous event. Hundreds of thousands of motorcycle riders make the trip twice a year to The World's Most Famous Beach. If you haven't yet been to Bike Week or Biketoberfest, you are really missing out on what makes Central Florida famous. If you ride your own motorcycle, you can cruise Main Street, Beach Street, and dozens of other main drag areas to show off your chrome. If you don't ride but still want to watch, get a table near one of the main drags and watch the action all day and night. If you really want to take part, most bike shops can teach you to ride before the next great pilgrimage!

officialbikeweek.com
biketoberfest.org

TIP
If you want to get out of the crowds for a longer excursion, the Daytona Regional Chamber of Commerce has plenty of great rides for you to experience the Florida back roads.

BONUS TIP
You may also want to check out Leesburg's Bike Fest. It's not quite as big but still great motorcycle fun.

GO TO A STATE PARK
ACCESSIBLE ONLY BY BOAT

Hontoon Island is located in the St. Johns River near DeLand and offers a nature experience second to none. Legend has it that early Native American settlers lived on this island thousands of years ago. You can still see the remnants of their activities scattered throughout the park. You do have to take a boat to get there, but overnight camping is available, so you can stay as long as you like.

2309 River Ridge Rd.
DeLand, FL 32720
(386) 736-5309
floridastateparks.org/hontoonisland

TIP
Check out the Owl Totem. The original totem pole was found in the water back in 1955 but has been taken to a museum. The replica marks a burial ground that dates back 3,300 years.

TAKE A TOUR OF THE HOLY LAND
(WITHOUT THE CHILDREN)

Sure, the children will love the Holy Land Experience theme park, but there is so much history to see and read about that it may be worth your time to spend an afternoon without them to get a deeper experience. The park is full of architecture that takes you back two thousand years to the time of Christ. There are live dramas throughout the day in the state-of-the-art Church of All Nations. If you are a fan of history, especially biblical history, this theme park right along Interstate-4 may surprise you.

4655 Vineland Rd.
Orlando, FL 32811
(407) 872-2272
holylandexperience.com

TIP
Take time to study the world's largest indoor model of Jerusalem. When you see how the city is laid out on a grand scale, you can understand biblical stories in a better way.

LEARN ABOUT BLACK HISTORY
AT THE WELLS' BUILT MUSEUM

Located in the community of Parramore in Orlando, the Wells' Built Museum of African American History and Culture tells the story of Central Florida's black residents, from the Civil War to the present day. The museum is actually an old hotel built in the 1920s by Dr. William Monroe Wells. The hotel served traveling African-Americans during the segregation era when blacks couldn't stay in the same hotels as whites. The six-thousand-square-foot museum features posters, magazines, artifacts, and art from Orlando's African-American community, along with some African art on loan from local collectors. Tours of the museum are also available.

511 W. South St.
Orlando, FL 32805
(407) 245-7535
wellsbuiltmuseum.com

TIP
If you're interested in black history, check out the Hannibal Square Heritage Center in Winter Park. The center is a tribute to Winter Park's historic African-American community.

FIND YOUR INNER PEACE
AT BOK TOWER

Bok Tower Gardens is a National Historic Landmark and attraction that has represented "authentic" Florida since 1929, but you can't understand how incredible this place is until you make the drive to Polk County. The tower stands in the middle of the beautiful gardens designed by world-famous landscape architect Frederick Law Olmsted, Jr. It is the perfect setting to relax, meditate, or simply enjoy the natural beauty of Florida, and when the "Singing Tower" springs to life, it is an experience your family won't soon forget. The 205-foot-tall Bok Tower is called the "Singing Tower" because it houses a sixty-bell carillon. The bells ring out every afternoon at 1:00 and 3:00 and fill the gardens with music that you have to hear to believe.

1151 Tower Blvd.
Lake Wales, FL 33853
(863) 676-1408
boktowergardens.org

TIP
If you love architecture, pay the extra money and tour the Pinewood Estate on the Bok Tower grounds.

DIVE BACK IN TIME
IN DEVIL'S DEN

Florida has some great offshore diving, but one of the best dives in the state is in landlocked Williston. One of North America's most ancient places, Devil's Den is an underground spring inside a dry cave. The spring is always seventy-two degrees, so it's cool in the summer and warm in the winter. The remains of many extinct animals from the Pleistocene Age (two million to ten thousand years ago) were discovered at Devil's Den, including bones of early man dating back to 75,000 BC. You don't have to be a diver to enjoy the Den: Snorkeling is also allowed. Devil's Den is truly a natural wonder and a step back in time a short drive north of Orlando.

5390 NE 180th Ave.
Williston, FL 32696
(352) 528-3344
devilsden.com

TIP
The water temperature is actually why it's called Devil's Den. On cool mornings, the steam comes billowing out of the cave's chimney, looking like smoke coming from deep within the earth. Get there early to see it.

SEE THE WHITE HOUSE...
IN CLERMONT

Let's face it. A trip to Washington, DC, can be time consuming and expensive. So if you've always wanted to see what the Oval Office looks like, just head to Clermont. The Presidents Hall of Fame is a tribute to all the things that make our government great. A variety of exhibits keep the children entertained, along with a bounty of historical information so that adults can learn, as well. There is even a tiny replica of the White House, so you can get a closer look at all the rooms of the executive mansion.

123 US 27
Clermont, FL 34711
(352) 394-2836
thepresidentshalloffame.com

TIP
There is even a replica of Mount Rushmore outside! The Discovery Channel thought this attraction was worth an entire show, so it's obviously worth a trip to Lake County to explore.

GET STARSTRUCK
AT THE ORLANDO SCIENCE CENTER

It's educational, it's entertaining, and it's indoors! The Orlando Science Center is one of the top science centers in the country, and for good reason. Four floors of thought-provoking exhibits and interactive shows take visitors on a science adventure that explores physics, biology, meteorology, archaeology, and engineering.

The Science Center's new KidsTown exhibit is designed for children ages seven and under and features eleven thousand square feet of activities. Children can invent, create, build, and make discoveries. The idea is that learning is fun.

777 E. Princeton St.
Orlando, FL 32803
(407) 514-2000
osc.org

TIP
During the new Science Night Live events, adults can learn about the wonders of science while sipping adult beverages.

OTHER MUSEUMS TO CHECK OUT IN ORLANDO

Orlando Fire Museum
orlandofiremuseum.org

Orange County Regional History Center
thehistorycenter.org

ROCK OUT
AT THE MONUMENT OF THE STATES

It may not sound very exciting, but a pyramid of stones from every single state is a pretty cool attraction. The Monument of the States stands in downtown Kissimmee, not far from the theme parks. This monument was reportedly started back in 1942, shortly after the attack on Pearl Harbor. Governors, state officials, residents, and even President Franklin Delano Roosevelt have all sent stones or slabs from their home states. Rocks from twenty-two other countries have also been added. The All States Tourist Club of Kissimmee mortared all the pieces together and then arranged them in a strange-looking formation, which stands around fifty feet high. The attraction was spruced up recently thanks to a $30 million renovation at Kissimmee's Lakefront Park. If you went a few years ago and it appeared "tired," it has been spruced up since then.

300 E. Monument Ave.
Kissimmee, FL 34741
(407) 847-2821

TIP
Look closely for the human bones!

GET SUDSY AT A SOAP MUSEUM
AT CLEAN THE WORLD

The first museum of its kind dedicated to soap is in Orlando at Clean the World, a nonprofit organization that recycles soap products from hotels worldwide. The Soap Story, an interactive museum that opened in 2018, tells the story of health and hygiene products through advertisements, illustrations, antique washing machines, and educational pieces. Some of the items date back to the early 1700s. Visitors will learn about some of the earliest soap brands and see products featuring popular name brands, such as Palmolive, Yardley, Ivory, Dial, Persil, Pears, and Tide. The museum is free, and you don't even have to wash behind your ears to enter.

2544 E. Landstreet Rd., Suite 600
Orlando, FL 32824
(407) 574-8353
cleantheworld.org

GET SPIRITUAL
IN THE "PSYCHIC CAPITAL OF THE WORLD"

If you are interested in the supernatural and the metaphysical, you owe it to yourself to check out the town of Cassadaga. Even if those types of spiritual endeavors don't appeal to you, you should see what the "Psychic Capital of the World" is all about. The town is populated with certified mediums and healers, and when you walk the few streets in the metaphysical district, you can truly feel something unique. Maybe it's the calmness that brings everyone down . . . or up . . . a level.

People come from all over the world to experience the Cassadaga Spiritualist Camp and to better understand spirituality. Only fifty-five residences are located in the historic district, with approximately thirty-five mediums living here. So if you want to rub elbows with people who talk with spirits and see the world in a different light, the services at Cassadaga Spiritualist Camp need to be on your list.

Cassadaga Spiritualist Camp
Bookstore
1112 Stevens St.
Cassadaga, FL 32706
(386) 228-2880
cassadaga.org

Cassadaga Hotel
355 Cassadaga Rd.
Cassadaga, FL 32706
(386) 228-2323
cassadagahotel.net

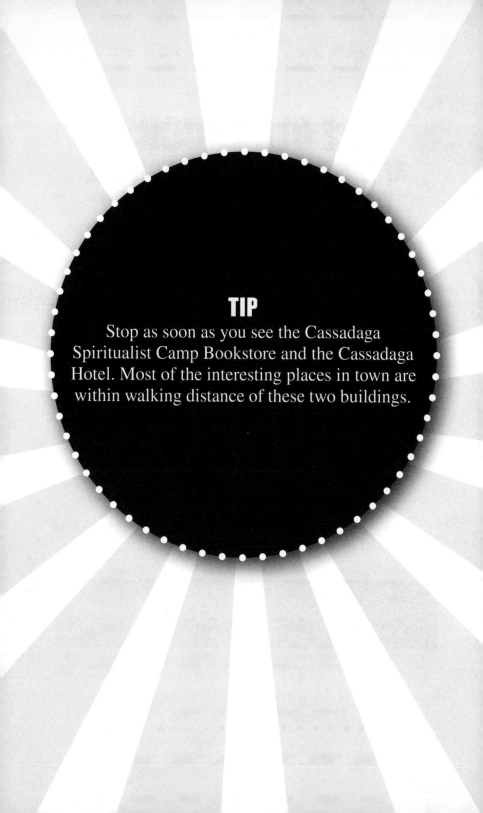

TIP

Stop as soon as you see the Cassadaga Spiritualist Camp Bookstore and the Cassadaga Hotel. Most of the interesting places in town are within walking distance of these two buildings.

SEE OLD TRUCKS
AT THE WASTE PRO HISTORICAL TRUCK MUSEUM IN SANFORD

The way garbage is collected has changed dramatically over time, and this museum in Sanford showcases that evolution. The Waste Pro Historical Truck Museum, located at the regional offices of Waste Pro, has on display a collection of original and restored antique waste collection trucks. Some of the prized vehicles include a 1926 GMC flatbed and a green 1946 Dodge truck. Many of the trucks in the collection have a connection to John Jennings, the founder of Waste Pro, one of the largest waste collection companies in the United States.

3705 St. Johns Pkwy.
Sanford, FL 32771
(407) 774-0800
wasteprousa.com

TIP
Go to the Waste Pro website to book a tour of the Waste Pro Historical Truck Museum before heading up to Sanford.

SHOOT AND KILL ZOMBIES
AT ZOMBIE OUTBREAK IN ORLANDO

Have you ever wondered whether you could survive a zombie apocalypse? There's only one way to find out, and that's at Zombie Outbreak, a 9,400-square-foot live action attraction on International Drive in Orlando. The *Night of the Living Dead* meets *Resident Evil* experience is like a real-life video game that gives you the chance to shoot and kill zombies, which are played by actors. Zombie Outbreak is set in a research facility overrun by the undead. You must go in locked and loaded with lifelike weapons that are made of metal and contain a CO_2 cartridge, creating a recoil when fired. (The guns shoot lasers.) The object is to make it through the nightmare without getting bitten. Good luck . . . you're gonna need it.

7364 International Dr.
Orlando, FL 32819
(407) 745-4068
zombieoutbreak.co/florida

GET UP CLOSE WITH AN EAGLE
AT THE AUDUBON CENTER FOR BIRDS OF PREY IN MAITLAND

Birds are majestic creatures, and they are even more stunning up close. The Audubon Center for Birds of Prey in Maitland is an urban environmental center that focuses on the rescue, medical treatment, rehabilitation, and release of Florida's raptors. (No, not the dinosaurs.) Raptors are birds such as hawks, eagles, falcons, owls, and ospreys that have keen eyesight and take their food by force. Founded in 1979, the Audubon Center for Birds of Prey has treated more than twenty thousand injured or orphaned birds of prey. Stop by the Center's Magic of Flight barn, which houses birds going through rehabilitation.

1101 Audubon Way
Maitland, FL 32751
(407) 644-0190
fl.audubon.org/chapters-centers/audubon-center-birds-prey

TIP
If you plan it right, you can visit the center in the spring during the Baby Owl Shower. Every year the center hosts the event to raise funds and awareness for its many baby patients.

DO A MOONLIGHT WALKING TOUR
AT GREENWOOD CEMETERY

The people who put Orlando on the map are buried at one of the city's most beautiful places, just south of downtown. Greenwood Cemetery is where the "who's who" of Orlando are laid to rest, and when the moon is full the place really comes to life . . . so to speak! The city-owned cemetery offers a stroll where you can see the tombstones of people who made Orlando what it is today. Such names as Parramore, Carr, Bumby, Robinson, Tinker, and others are all buried on the peaceful grounds. Tours are led by a local historian, so you will walk away from a night among the dead with a new appreciation for the City Beautiful.

1603 Greenwood St.
Orlando, FL 32801
(407) 246-2616
greenwood-cemetery.net

TIP
The moonlight strolls are generally limited to fifty people.
When you see one on the calendar, sign up quickly!

SEE THE OVIEDO GHOST LIGHTS

Some say the ghostly lights don't exist. Others swear they are real, although it's hard to describe exactly what they are. The mysterious lights are called the Oviedo Ghost Lights, and people have been spotting them for decades. They can allegedly be seen at the County Road 419 Bridge over the Econlockhatchee River between Chuluota and Oviedo. People who have seen them say they look like balls of light that hover over the road. In some spottings, the lights even reportedly chased cars and then disappeared. You may not see them every time, but it's worth the night drive to see what you can find.

Highway 419
East of Oviedo at the Econ River Bridge

TIP
Most spottings happen during warmer months. That may make sense if the lights are in fact glowing swamp gases being released by the earth.

WATCH YOUR CAR ROLL "UPHILL"
AT SPOOK HILL

This mysterious hill has become a legend around the world, and it's located right here in our own backyard. "Spook Hill" is in Lake Wales, southwest of Kissimmee. On this stretch of road, when you park and put your car in neutral, it appears to roll uphill. There is such a big legend surrounding Spook Hill that the city has put up signs to guide you there. I could explain how it happens, but that would ruin the fun of experiencing it yourself.

lakewaleschamber.com/spook-hill

TIP
If you are leaving from Orlando, this is a pretty long drive. You may want to find another activity on the bucket list in that area and make it part of a bigger trip.

BE WITH BUTTERFLIES
AT LUKAS NURSERY IN OVIEDO

This may be the best chance in all of Central Florida to be around butterflies. The four-thousand-square-foot, one-of-a-kind attraction in Oviedo lets you feed butterflies from your fingertips. The Butterfly Encounter is one of the largest butterfly conservatories in the state of Florida. Though open year-round, the attraction's peak season is from April to September. Besides the butterflies, small birds, such as quail and finches, also call the Butterfly Encounter home. Connected to the Butterfly Encounter is the Urban Farmhouse Gift Shop, where you can meet all your butterfly needs, including butterfly art.

1909 Slavia Rd.
Oviedo, FL 32765
(407) 738-4319
lukasnursery.com

TIP
Lukas Nursery is one of the best spots in all of Central Florida to buy plants and flowers. After finishing the Butterfly Encounter, walk around and pick up a plant to take home.

RIDE A GLASS-BOTTOMED BOAT
AT SILVER SPRINGS

Silver Springs State Park is one of the most beautiful places on the planet and has to be seen to be truly understood. Seven major springs here pump out 550 million gallons of water a day. The best way to see "Florida's Oldest Attraction" is on board the world-famous glass-bottomed boats. This attraction near Ocala has been drawing crowds since the 1800s and is even the beautiful backdrop for such movies as *Creature from the Black Lagoon* and *Tarzan*. The waters are billed as 99.8 percent pure, so it's as close to perfection as you can get.

5656 E. Silver Springs Blvd.
Silver Springs, FL 34488
(352) 261-5840
silversprings.com

TIP
Watch old videos of the *Sea Hunt* TV show to build the anticipation. Many parts of the series were shot on location here.

SHOPPING AND FASHION

PICK STRAWBERRIES
IN LAKE COUNTY

It may sound like a lot of work, but strawberry picking in Lake County is actually a lot of fun. You can pick the fresh fruit in many places, but one of the favorites is Oak Haven Farms near Sorrento. It's free to get in, but, of course, you have to pay for your berries once you're done.

Oak Haven also has a small zipline for the children, a play area, and a tractor ride that takes you around the old homestead. After you're done picking and playing, you can get hot dogs to roast by the fire and some of the best strawberry milkshakes you've ever tasted. If you really want to do it right, grab a strawberry shortcake to go along with your fine dining!

32418 Avington Rd.
Sorrento, FL 32776
(352) 735-1996
berriesandwines.com

TIP
The baskets the farm hands out hold a lot of berries! You will likely pick more than you can eat, so be careful.

GO TO FLORIDA'S NEWEST "SPRING"

Almost everyone can find something fun to do at Disney Springs. The sprawling outdoor complex features more than a hundred shops, bars, restaurants, entertainment spots, and activities. Known as Downtown Disney for more than a decade, Disney Springs officially opened in 2016 after a three-year renovation. Such global brands as UGG, Zara, Levi's, and others surround the man-made spring in the middle of the complex. Celebrity chefs Art Smith, Masaharu Morimoto, and Rick Bayless also operate restaurants at Disney Springs. There's no cost to get in, and parking is free too.

1486 Buena Vista Dr.
Orlando, FL 32830
(407) 939-6244
disneysprings.com

BUY LOCAL
AT THE WINTER PARK FARMERS' MARKET

There is no better way to feed your family right while helping the local economy at the same time. The Winter Park Farmers' Market is truly a treat every Saturday morning. Dozens of vendors display their wares, baked goods, fresh fruits, and vegetables while shoppers stroll along the streets around the Old Train Depot. This is Florida living at its finest. Many people bring the dogs, grab a cup of coffee, and get their fresh produce for the week ahead. But even if you're not in the mood to buy, just walking around the Winter Park Farmers' Market and taking in the sights and smells is a treat.

200 W. New England Ave.
Winter Park, FL 32789
(407) 599-3397
cityofwinterpark.org/departments/parks-recreation/farmers-market

---

TIP
Start a family tradition and buy the kettle corn every weekend!

OTHER FARMERS' MARKETS OF NOTE

Downtown Clermont Farmers' Market
clermontdowntownpartnership.com

Lake Mary Farmers' Market
lakemaryfarmersmarket.com

Orlando Farmers' Market at Lake Eola Park
orlandofarmersmarket.com

Winter Garden Farmers' Market
wintergardenfarmersmarket.com

GO ANTIQUING
AT RENNINGER'S VINTAGE ANTIQUE CENTER

If you're in the market for a couch from the 1930s or a piece of turn-of-the-century jewelry, there is no better place in Central Florida to find it than at Renninger's Vintage Antique Center. Located in Mount Dora, about thirty miles northwest of Orlando, Renninger's Vintage Antique Center is one of the largest places like it in the US. Every weekend more than 180 dealers set up inside the forty-thousand-square-foot, air-conditioned indoor market. There's also a flea and farmers' market on the 117-acre site.

20651 US 441
Mount Dora, FL 32757
(352) 383-8393
renningers.net

TIP
Try to make it out during the Collector's Extravaganza, a three-times-a-year event where more than eight hundred dealers sell their wares.

HANG TEN
AT RON JON SURF SHOP

Contrary to popular belief, Ron Jon Surf Shop didn't start in Cocoa Beach, but it certainly made the city famous. The store is recognized as the largest surfing shop in the world and is a mecca for surfers from across the globe. Even if you are not a surfer, it's hard to say you've "done it all" when you haven't checked this one off the list. You can always buy a pair of sunglasses and shorts so that you can at least look the part!

4151 N. Atlantic Ave.
Cocoa Beach, FL 32931
(321) 799-8888
ronjonsurfshop.com

TIP
While you're in Cocoa Beach, you will also want to drive a little farther down the beach and see the Kelly Slater statue commemorating the local dude who just happens to be the most famous surfer in history.

VISIT AN ICONIC BUILDING
AT ORANGE WORLD

It's an orange. It's a souvenir shop. It's both! Orange World in Kissimmee is dubbed the "World's Largest Orange" and sells a variety of Florida-themed goods, including fresh oranges. During certain times of the year, look for Florida-grown honeybells, ruby red grapefruits, navel oranges, valencia oranges, and tangerines. If you're not interested in fruit, Orange World also has many Florida-made candies and treats, as well as T-shirts, hats, and all kinds of other Florida-based souvenirs. Don't forget to get your picture in front of the building because, well, it's a big orange and would look great on Instagram.

5395 W. Irlo Bronson Memorial Hwy.
Kissimmee, FL 34746
(800) 531-3182
orangeworld192.com

TIP
Orange World sometimes gives out free samples of its fruit, so if you're lucky you may get to sample a slice of orange or grapefruit before buying a bag.

TAKE A MONSTER TRUCK TOUR
OF ORANGE GROVES

This is one of those "only in Florida" roadside attractions that you simply have to see to believe. The 4x4 Monster Truck Adventure is a tour in a modified school bus with gigantic tires of the Showcase of Citrus, a working, citrus farm and cattle ranch in Lake County. During the 4x4 Adventure, you'll ride through native woodland, pasture land, grove land, and swamp land while learning about Florida history. Open everyday of the year, Showcase of Citrus also features farm animals, wine tastings and a country store.

5010 US Hwy. 27
Clermont, FL 34714
(352) 394-4377
showcaseofcitrus.com

TIP
It's not just a tour of orange groves. The tour also takes you off-road into swampy areas, so be ready for a fun ride.

FIND A VINYL GEM
AT A CENTRAL FLORIDA RECORD STORE

Vinyl is back! OK, records never really went anywhere, but there's certainly been a resurgence of vinyl in the past few years. Central Florida is one of the best places in the country to find new and used records. Whether you're looking for a rare, original pressing of Miles Davis' *Kind of Blue* or the latest seven-inch from an Orlando-based punk rock band, be sure to check out such local shops as Park Avenue CDs, Uncle Tony's Donut Shoppe, Rock & Roll Heaven, East West Music, and Foundation. And for the true vinyl newbie, some of the shops sell turntables.

TIP
Besides the brick-and-mortar shops, several local flea markets, thrift stores, and antique centers carry vinyl records.

RECORD SHOPS IN CENTRAL FLORIDA

Park Avenue CDs
2916 Corrine Dr.
Orlando, FL 32803
(407) 447-7275
parkavecds.com

Uncle Tony's Donut Shoppe
703 N. Orange Ave.
Orlando, FL 32801
(407) 734-0034
eldonutshoppe.com

Rock & Roll Heaven
1814 N. Orange Ave.
Orlando, FL 32804
(407) 896-1952
rock-n-rollheaven.com

East West Music & More
4895 S. Orange Ave.
Orlando, FL 32806
(407) 859-8991

Foundation College Park
2529 Edgewater Dr.
Orlando, FL 32804
(407) 502-8627
instagram.com/
foundationcollegepark

Re-Runz Records
310 S. Orange Blossom Trail
Orlando, FL 32805
(407) 413-5059
rerunzrecords.com

Triangle Vinyl
1208 Bowman St.
Clermont, FL 34711
(407) 408-5751
trianglevinyl.com

Remix Record Shop
1217 N. Mills Ave.
Orlando, FL 32803
(407) 801-5300
remixthestore.com

TOUR A LOCAL FARM
AT LAKE MEADOW NATURALS

The city is great, but sometimes you have to get back to the farm. Lake Meadow Naturals is a hundred-acre working farm that specializes in humanely raised natural meats and cage-free chickens. Many area restaurants feature products from Lake Meadow Naturals. The farm hosts one-hour guided tours (minimum of six people, Tuesday–Friday), where you can see the animals and learn about the products made on the farm. The store at Lake Meadow Naturals is open six days a week and sells many homemade products, including jams and jellies, pickle products, and fermented products.

10000 Mark Adam Rd.
Ocoee, FL 34761
(321) 206-6262
lakemeadownaturals.com

PLANT YOURSELF
AT THE PLANT STREET MARKET

Do you want to do yoga, drink a beer, or buy a filet mignon? At the Plant Street Market in downtown Winter Garden, you can do all three (and lots more). This community-minded market features more than twenty vendors selling handmade goods and natural organic foods. It's a great place to stop in for a bite to eat and a tasty adult beverage. The market is attached to the Crooked Can Brewing Company, an on-site brewery and taproom. Stop in on Sundays from noon to 4:00 p.m. for a tour of the brewery. The Plant Street Market also has a pet-friendly patio and live entertainment.

426 W. Plant St.
Winter Garden, FL 34787
(786) 671-1748
crookedcan.com/plant-st-market

TIP
Another great market is East End Market in Orlando's Audubon Park Garden District. The market is home to lots of funky shops and Gideon's Bakehouse, quite possibly the best cookie maker in the world.

SUGGESTED
ITINERARIES

THEME PARKS

Take a Hidden Tour of Walt Disney World, 24

Explore Somewhere, Beyond the Sea (World), 25

Visit a New Theme Park in an Old Location, 28

Just Do Fun Spot America Already!, 58

Take a Tour of the Holy Land (without the Children), 103

Wrestle a Gator (Sort Of), 86

INDOOR ADVENTURES

See the Shuttle Atlantis, Dings and All, 92

Get Ice! at Gaylord Palms, 94

Love the Blues at Blue Man Group, 34

See the White House . . . in Clermont, 107

Go Skiing at WinterClub Indoor Ski & Snowboard in Winter Park, 79

Get Starstruck at the Orlando Science Center, 108

Scale an Indoor Mountain at Aiguille Rock Climbing Center, 66

OUTDOOR EXPEDITIONS

Watch the Sea Cows at Blue Spring, 52

Go Back in Time on the Dora Canal, 53

Paddleboard along Turner Flats, 55

DATE NIGHT

ACTIVITIES
BY REGION

ORLANDO (CENTRAL)

Cheer on Orlando's Sports Teams, 56

Do a Moonlight Walking Tour at Greenwood Cemetery, 117

Paddle the Swan Boats at Lake Eola, 60

Celebrate Christmas Year-Round at Frosty's Christmastime Lounge, 12

NORTH

Polka at Willow Tree, 96

See "Lady Liberty" at Big Tree Park, 62

Pick Strawberries in Lake County, 124

Zip the Canyons Like Superman in Ocala, 72

Cook Your Own Pancakes at De Leon Springs, 8

Dive Back in Time in Devil's Den, 106

Ride a Glass-Bottomed Boat at Silver Springs, 121

SOUTH

Find Your Inner Peace at the Bok Tower, 105

Rock Out at the Monument of the States, 110

Go Hang Gliding in "Flat" Kissimmee, 75

Take a Monster Truck Tour of Orange Groves, 131

Go Up, Up, and Away in a Hot Air Balloon, 48

BEACHES

ACTIVITIES
BY SEASON

(Yes, we know there aren't really seasons!)

WINTER

Ride a Glass-Bottomed Boat at Silver Springs, 121

Watch the Sea Cows at Blue Spring, 52

Do a Moonlight Walking Tour at Greenwood Cemetery, 117

Take a Monster Truck Tour of Orange Groves, 131

SPRING

Be with Butterflies at Lukas Nursery in Oviedo, 120

Go Behind the Scenes at the Daytona International Speedway, 63

Tour a Local Farm at Lake Meadow Naturals, 134

Dive Back in Time in Devil's Den, 106

Celebrate America's Pastime at a Spring Training Game, 64

SUMMER

Watch Disappearing Island Appear, 30

Escape for a Day to Wekiva Island, 46

Paddleboard along Turner Flats, 55

Everything else unless it's too hot!

FALL

Go Veg in Central Florida, 10

Get Ice! at Gaylord Palms, 94

Cheer on Orlando's Sports Teams, 56

INDEX